The Library of Intergenerational Learning

Native Americans™

Zuni Children and Elders Talk Together

E. Barrie Kavasch

The Rosen Publishing Group's
PowerKids Press™
New York

To the Zuni People—to their amazing history and bright future!

Published in 1999 by The Rosen Publishing Group, Inc.
29 East 21st Street, New York, NY 10010

First Edition

Book Design: Danielle Primiceri

Photo Credits: Cover and all inside photos by A.J. Group, John Bacolo.

Kavasch, E. Barrie.
    Zuni children and elders talk together/by E. Barrie Kavasch.
        p.   cm.—(Library of intergenerational learning. Native Americans)
    Summary: Explores the culture and traditions of the Zuni people through the voices
    of their children and older people.
    ISBN 0-8239-5227-4
    1. Zuni Indians—Juvenile literature. [1. Zuni Indians. 2. Indians of North America—New Mexico.] I. Title. II. Series.
    Kavasch, E. Barrie. Library of intergenerational learning. Native Americans.
    E99.Z9.K38 1997
    306'.089'979—dc21   97-49266
                                                                            CIP
                                                                            AC

Manufactured in the United States of America

Contents

I Am Zuni

"My name is Vance Goston Booqua. I am Zuni, and I am seven years old. I like to tell funny vampire jokes. Most of all I like to ride my bike through the streets and lots around Halona Plaza in Zuni **pueblo** (PWEH-bloh). The pueblo is where we live."

The Zuni lived in the southwestern regions of the United States for thousands of years. Today, most of the Zuni live in Zuni, New

Here, Vance (far left) plays the Money Game with his friends. These kids made the game themselves.

Mexico, on their **reservations** (reh-zer-VAY-shunz).

Even though the world is changing around them, the Zuni never forget how important their **culture** (KUL-cher) and **traditions** (truh-DISH-unz) are to their people and especially to their children. The children are always learning about their culture and history from their elders and parents.

"I'm Lindrick Baker, and I'm eight. I like to ride my bike with my friends. Sometimes we have races to see who can ride the fastest, and who can run the fastest too. We also like to learn special things from our elders."

Zuni kids often ride their bikes and play in the shadow of the sacred Corn Mountain.

5

Clans

Michael Calavaza is twelve years old. He is Parrot, or Macaw, **Clan** (KLAN). A clan is a large group of related people. There are many clans in one tribe, and all of the people in a clan are related. Zuni children inherit the clan of their mothers. This means that Michael's mom is also Parrot Clan.

"I help my mom by taking care of my baby brother," Michael says. "His name is Kallen, and he's eleven months old. My mom works really hard. She owns a restaurant called The Backyard Cafe. She's also an artist. I like to draw and work with pottery, just like my mom.

"My grandparents say that women are the most important part of Zuni culture, and are very important to all of our people. I know that my mom is very important to me. She teaches me a lot."

Michael's pet parrot is called a macaw. It is a living symbol and reminder of his clan. ▶

Celebrations

The Zuni celebrate many things in life. God, nature, and the spirits of their **ancestors** (AN-ses-terz) are **honored** (ON-erd) in every celebration.

"I learned how to weave in high school," says Marcus Banketewa. "I made my own frame loom and weaving tools from willow tree wood. I like the way different colors blend and work together when I weave. And I enjoy sharing my craft, especially with children."

Some of the belts and sashes woven by Marcus are worn by **kachina** (kuh-CHEE-nuh) dancers in Zuni celebrations. "My cousin Gilligan and I wear the sashes when we are Eagle Dancers. The canes and dance sticks that we carve and paint are another way that we celebrate our Zuni culture. Some of our artwork is displayed in galleries and museums around the country."

The belt that Marcus weaves here is a traditional Zuni belt. It can be worn by men or women.

An Elder's Story

The Zuni elders are well-respected. They are the ones who teach the younger **generations** (jen-er-AY-shunz) about Zuni history and the ways of the world. The elders are respected for their experience and knowledge. Peter Pinicion is one of the elders in the Zuni pueblo.

"I am Corn Clan, and I am 64 years old. I work as a silversmith and a jeweler, but I have always been interested in arrowheads. I love finding old arrowheads, but when I was younger I wanted to see if I could make them. I taught myself how to shape them using

Peter Pinicion has been making arrowheads for a long time. He knows the importance of sharing this craft with others.

simple tools. I often sell them at the trading post where I sometimes show people how to make them. I also enjoy teaching flint knapping, which is tap-ping stone to make fine tools.

"I like to teach at the **A:shiwi A:wan** (ah-SHEE-wee ah-WAN) Museum and **Her-itage** (HAYR-ih-tij) Center on Main Street in Zuni. Working with young people and sharing my craft makes me feel good. Sometimes I tell stories about Zuni life while I teach."

▲

Here you can see Peter making arrowheads with his simple tools. A finished arrowhead is thin and has a sharp point.

The Land

The Zuni reservation was formed over one hundred years ago in 1877, but Zuni people have been living in the Southwest for more than 2,000 years. Their land includes 636 miles around the Zuni Pueblo in Zuni, New Mexico. The Zuni people are still working to reclaim land that was taken by the United States government. More than two million acres of land were taken in the past 100 years.

These Zuni kachina dolls represent the connection between the land and the kachina spirits.

Zuni lands are beautiful, **ancient** (AYN-shent), and **sacred** (SAY-kred). There are many special places where Zuni **ceremonies** (SEHR-eh-moh-neez) are privately performed. One of the most important places is the sacred Corn Mountain, or Zuni Mountain. Special kachina dances take place outside with the sacred mountain in the background. **Pilgrimages** (PIL-grih-mij-ez) are also made to Corn Mountain. This mountain is a sacred background to life on the Zuni reservation.

The Zuni are famous for their farming in the dry desert areas where they live. Some of their crops include corn, squash, beans, and cotton. Zuni people today also create fine jewelry and artwork.

Families

"I am Rita Edaakie. My grandsons and their friends created the Nawetsa Dance Group. They have performed our traditional Zuni dances at the big Apache Ceremonial in Mescalero, New Mexico. I am so proud of them."

Rita works at the A:shiwi A:wan Museum and Heritage Center in Zuni. She does craft work with children and families of the pueblo. In Zuni culture, the family is the base from which everything else grows. So the Center brings together families to teach and share their customs. One favorite activity is sewing the clan **symbols** (SIM-bulz) on fabric.

"The center allows us to bring together the living Zuni generations with the ways of our ancestors," says Rita. "We enjoy honoring families and their talents. We believe that this creates a bond that keeps folks together and teaches our children."

◄ *Rita likes to show her students different Zuni crafts. She hopes that someday her students will share these crafts with others.*

15

Kachinas

Kachinas represent special Zuni spirits and are a big part of Zuni culture. Masked dancers who become each kachina often go into sacred underground meeting places called kivas. There they rest and bless the kiva. They also get ready for the dances there. **Mudheads** (MUD-heds) are some of the special masked dancers, or clowns, who warn people when they are being bad. Mudheads are one of the forces that keep the clan **system** (SIS-tem) in place.

"My father, Alex Seowtewa, has been painting Zuni kachina murals, or wall paintings inside the Our Lady of Guadalupe Church in the pueblo for more than twenty years," says Edwin Seowtewa. "It takes a long time to paint just one figure. So my brothers and I help our father paint. We are proud to share our culture with others."

Most kachinas represent a different spirit in nature, such as the corn kachina and the snow kachina.

Food and Prayers

The making and baking of dough into bread is like a ceremony, or a prayer. It is done slowly and with lots of care, much like the prayers offered to Zuni ancestors and spirits. Zuni prayers always remember the children and elders and the importance of every family is honored. The elders and the holy people also pray that the Zuni will stay healthy and strong in their culture and traditions.

"My name is Roberta Banketewa. My sisters and I make a lot of bread dough to bake in the outdoor oven, or **horno** (HOR-noh). Usually we don't use all five ovens at one time. Today, we are building a fire in just one oven to bake more than twenty loaves of bread. It's hard work to build a hot fire and then wait for it to die down. We must brush away the coals and test the oven for just the right heat. Then we place the dough inside to be baked. Our bread is so delicious!"

◀ *Baking bread in the* hornos *is hot, hard work. Sometimes Roberta will shape the dough into animals before baking.*

19

Language

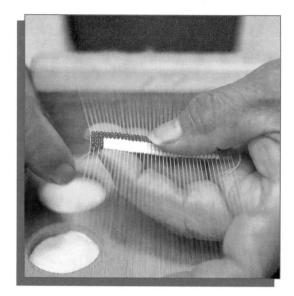

"Our language is the **foundation** (fown-DAY-shun) of our culture," says Rachel Weahkee. "I often teach my beadwork classes in our Zuni language. This way, our traditional crafts are blended with our language. We are closely related to the other Pueblo cultures, such as the Acoma and the Hopi. But the Zuni language is different. In our own language we call ourselves A:shiwi, which means 'the people.'"

"I am a beadwork artist. Here we are making small beaded dolls. I also teach loom beading. It is very important to concentrate when you are beading. It is also important to start learning the craft when you are young."

Rachel Weahkee is 72 years old. She has been doing beadwork since she was very young. ▶

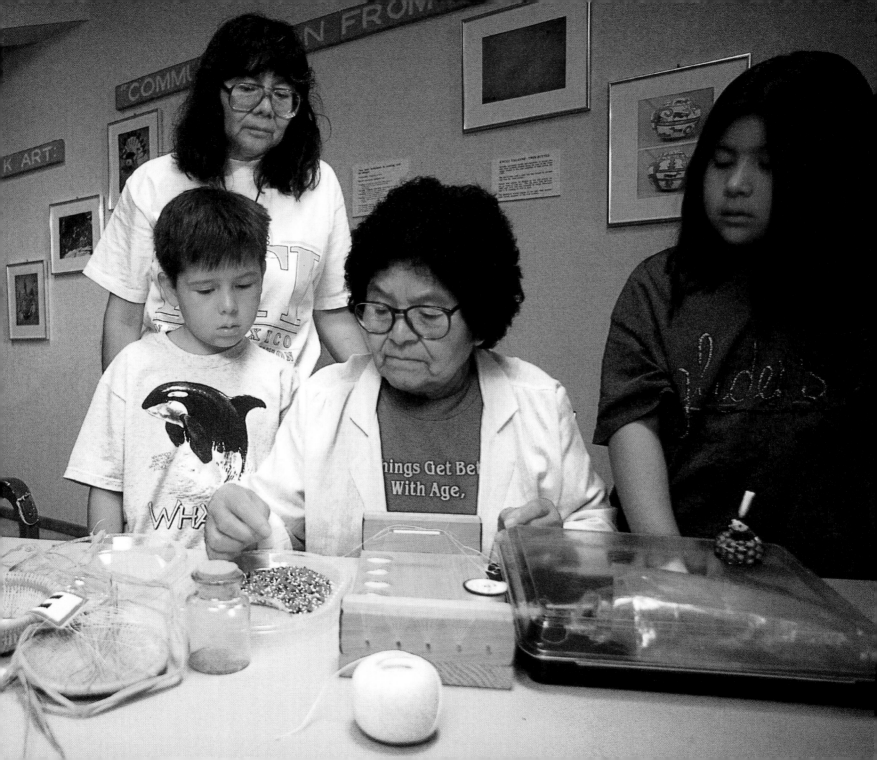

Future

The Zuni are proud of their rich traditional life. But they never forget that the future of the Zuni people lie in their children. "Working hard is important for all Zuni," says Michael Calavaza's mom, Desiree. "We all want to make a good life for our children." The Calavaza's family restaurant is called the Backyard Cafe. Soon it will also be an art gallery and a place where young Zuni artists can paint.

"Our people are talented in many ways. We work together to build a brighter future for all of us."

Glossary

ancestor (AN-ses-ter) A relative who lived long before you.

ancient (AYN-shent) Very old; from a long time ago.

A:shiwi A:wan (ah-SHEE-wee ah-WAN) The name of the Zuni heritage center in Zuni, New Mexico; A:shiwi also means "the people."

ceremony (SEHR-eh-moh-nee) A special activity done at certain times.

clan (KLAN) A group of people who are related within a tribe.

culture (KUL-cher) The beliefs, customs, art, and religions of a group of people.

foundation (fown-DAY-shun) The strong part on which other parts are built.

generation (jen-er-AY-shun) People born in the same period of time.

heritage (HAYR-ih-tij) The cultural traditions that are handed down from parent to child.

honor (ON-er) To show admiration and respect for someone.

horno (HOR-noh) A dome-shaped oven of mud and stone; sometimes called an adobe.

kachina (kuh-CHEE-nuh) A special spirit or a likeness of one.

mudhead (MUD-hed) Masked dancers that warn people of bad behavior.

pilgrimage (PIL-grih-mij) A journey to a sacred place.

pueblo (PWEH-bloh) A Southwest Indian village; the Spanish word for village.

reservation (reh-zer-VAY-shun) An area of land set aside by the government for the Native Americans to live on.

sacred (SAY-kred) Something that is highly respected and considered very important.

symbol (SIM-bul) A design that stands for something else.

system (SIS-tem) An orderly way of getting things done.

tradition (truh-DISH-un) To do things the way a group of people has done them for a long time.

Index